THE GOOD AND EASY

COOKBOOK

Breakfasts, Bag Lunches, Dinners, and Snacks

D1511179

Jean Bunnell
illustrated by Donna Stackhouse

J. Weston Walch, Publisher
Portland Maine

1   2   3   4   5   6   7   8   9   10

ISBN 0-8251-2395-X

Copyright © 1993
J Weston Walch, Publisher
P.O Box 658 • Portland, Maine 04104-0658

Printed in the United States of America

About This Book

It is exciting to move to an apartment and start living independently But for many people, this move also means taking on the new responsibility of preparing meals Frozen dinners are all right for a while—and one can go to the fast-food outlets from time to time But for variety and economy as well as good nutrition and the satisfaction it brings, basic food preparation skills are essential for independent living

This book includes 50 recipes offering a variety of main dishes, meats, vegetables and salads, sandwiches, breads, and desserts. Most recipes use fewer than five ingredients; none use more than nine The needed ingredients and utensils are listed clearly for each recipe. Step-by-step directions guide the beginning cook from start to finish

Additional materials will help with setting up a kitchen Lists include basic foods needed, as well as helpful utensils Tips are also included for food storage

Many of the recipes in this collection are included in two week-long menus shown on pages xviii–xxi The menus suggest foods to be eaten for three meals each day, as well as snacks. All of the recipes make enough for two, and so the portions in the menus can be doubled for four people

A food shopping guide accompanies each weekly menu

Contents

Part 6. Desserts 57

Index 67

Welcome!

Imagine making your favorite foods when you have a taste for them. How nice your home will smell when you bake cookies or a meat loaf!

With this step-by-step cookbook, you'll learn to prepare simple, delicious foods. And you'll add a lot to your life.

You'll add new freedom. When you're the cook, you can eat what you want, when you want, and where you want.

You'll add fun. Making meals and snacks is not just practical, it's creative and satisfying, too.

You'll save some money. Preparing your own meals can be much cheaper than ordering pizza or eating at fast-food places.

You'll look and feel better, and you'll have more energy. Shopping for your own food means you can choose plenty of healthful fruits, vegetables, and grains.

You'll feel proud. Picture yourself serving a tasty meal—one that you made yourself—to a friend or family member. Preparing meals at home gives you a special way of sharing.

Try the recipes in this book. You'll learn to make casseroles, sandwiches, salads, sweets, and other good foods. You'll gain useful cooking skills you'll always be glad to have. And you'll eat well, too. Enjoy!

A Guide to Daily Food Choices

Our bodies need a variety of foods each day. This chart shows how much to eat of different kinds of foods.

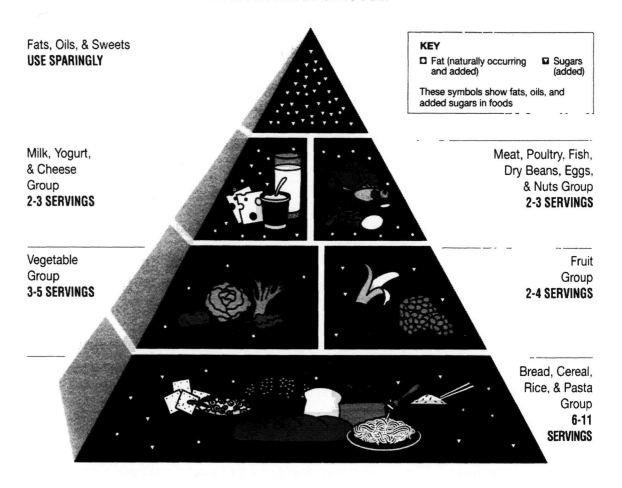

Fats, Oils, & Sweets
USE SPARINGLY

KEY
☐ Fat (naturally occurring and added)   ◪ Sugars (added)

These symbols show fats, oils, and added sugars in foods

Milk, Yogurt, & Cheese Group
2-3 SERVINGS

Meat, Poultry, Fish, Dry Beans, Eggs, & Nuts Group
2-3 SERVINGS

Vegetable Group
3-5 SERVINGS

Fruit Group
2-4 SERVINGS

Bread, Cereal, Rice, & Pasta Group
6-11 SERVINGS

Food Guide Pyramid

When choosing food, try to remember this guide. Your body needs:

- 6 to 11 servings of bread, cereal, rice, or pasta

- 3 to 5 servings of vegetables (beans, peas, broccoli, cabbage, etc.)

- 2 to 4 servings of fruit (oranges, apples, bananas, peaches, etc.)

- 2 to 3 servings of milk, yogurt, or cheese

- 2 to 3 servings of meat, poultry, fish, dried beans, eggs, or nuts

- small amounts of fats, oils, and sugars.

Basic Food Supplies for Your Kitchen

Get started in your kitchen with these basic food supplies.

Perishable Items	
milk juice eggs bread margarine potatoes onions	
Baking Supplies	
flour sugar cooking oil	
Grains	
cereal crackers instant rice	

Canned Goods	
soup tuna	
Herbs and Spices	
salt pepper parsley oregano garlic powder	
Condiments	
mustard relish ketchup	
Other	
peanut butter jelly salad dressing mayonnaise	

Food Storage Tips

Storing food correctly will keep it usable and safe to eat for a longer period of time.

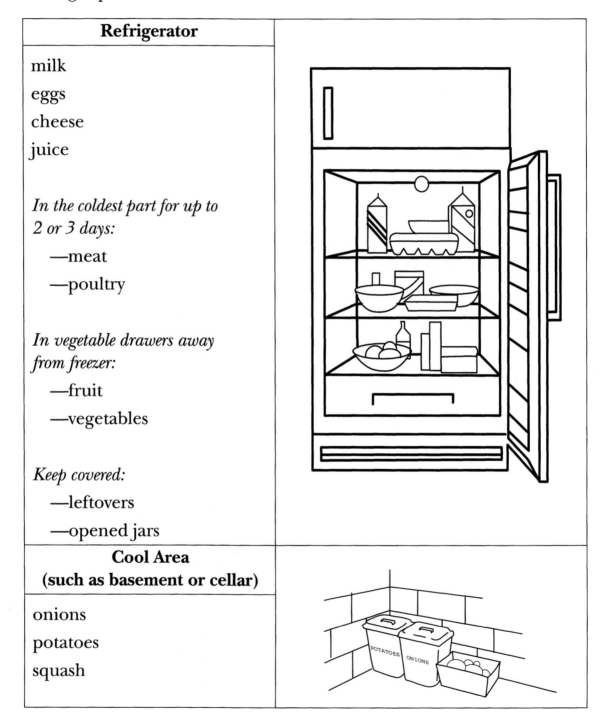

Refrigerator	
milk	
eggs	
cheese	
juice	
In the coldest part for up to 2 or 3 days:	
—meat	
—poultry	
In vegetable drawers away from freezer:	
—fruit	
—vegetables	
Keep covered:	
—leftovers	
—opened jars	
Cool Area (such as basement or cellar)	
onions	
potatoes	
squash	

Freezer	

frozen vegetables
 	
fruit juice concentrates
 	
Can be frozen in store wrap for up to 2 weeks:
   —meat
   —poultry
	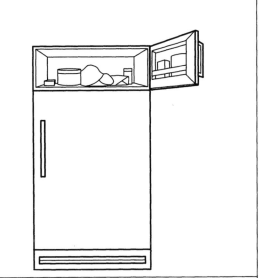

Cupboard	

baking supplies:
   flour
   sugar
   cooking oil
   spices
   herbs
unopened jars and cans
packaged food
peanut butter
pancake syrup
crackers
spaghetti/noodles
	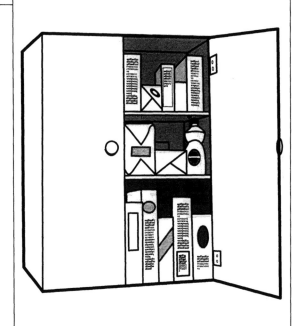

Basic Utensils for Your Kitchen

These basic utensils will be a help as you start preparing your own food.

wooden spoon

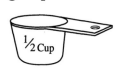

measuring cup

bowl

mixing spoons

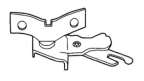

can opener

bread knife

measuring spoons

vegetable peeler

paring knife

spatula

vegetable grater

skillet

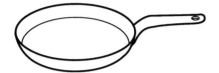

saucepan with cover

square baking dish

loaf pan

baking sheet

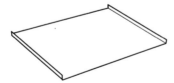

cutting board

muffin pan

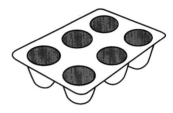

small casserole dish

pot holders

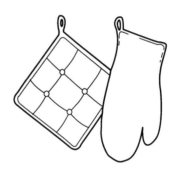

also: wax paper
    plastic bags
    paper towels
    aluminum foil

Menu for Week A

	DAY 1	DAY 2	DAY 3
Breakfast	Cereal with milk Banana	Fruit juice (1 cup) Toast Hard-boiled egg (page 41)	English muffin with peanut butter $\frac{1}{2}$ grapefruit
Lunch	Veggie hero sandwich (page 49) Apple Crispy crunchy bar (page 62)	Veggie hero sandwich Orange Crispy crunchy bar	Meat loaf sandwich Carrot sticks Banana Crispy crunchy bar
Snacks	Popcorn Orange	Bagel Banana	Popcorn Apple
Dinner	Oven-fried chicken (page 25) Cheesy potato puffs (page 29) Green beans ($\frac{1}{2}$ 10-oz. package) Crispy crunchy bar	Meat loaf (page 23) Stuffed baked potato (page 35) Mixed vegetables ($\frac{1}{2}$ 10-oz. package) Pudding parfait (page 65)	Pigs in a blanket (page 13) Mixed vegetables ($\frac{1}{2}$ 10-oz. package) Pudding parfait

(continued)

Menu for Week A *(continued)*

DAY 4	DAY 5	DAY 6	DAY 7
Applesauce ($\frac{1}{2}$ cup) Cinnamon toast (page 54) Milk (1 cup)	Bagel with jelly Apple Milk (1 cup)	Pancakes with syrup (page 12) Fruit juice (1 cup)	Fruit juice (1 cup) Scrambled eggs (page 16) Toast
Meat loaf sandwich Carrot sticks Orange 2 chocolate chip cookies (page 60)	Veggie hero sandwich Banana 2 chocolate chip cookies	Lasagna (leftover from day 5) Sliced tomato on lettuce leaves 2 chocolate chip cookies	Pizza bagels (page 44) Potato sticks Applesauce ($\frac{1}{2}$ cup) with cinnamon
Popcorn Orange	Muffin Apple	English muffin Banana	English muffin Apple
Spanish rice (page 19) Green beans ($\frac{1}{2}$ 10-oz. package) Muffin (page 56) Fruit salad (page 31)	Lasagna (page 10) Garlic roll (page 55) Tossed salad (page 36) Chocolate cream pie (page 61)	Pineapple baked beans and franks (page 14) Coleslaw (page 30) Muffin Chocolate cream pie	Chicken pie (page 4) Tossed salad Chocolate cream pie

Menu for Week B

	DAY 1	DAY 2	DAY 3
Breakfast	Toaster waffles with syrup Fruit juice	English muffin with jelly Fruit juice	Cereal with milk Strawberries
Lunch	Egg salad sandwich (page 41) Carrot sticks Apple 2 no-bake chocolate oatmeal cookies (page 64)	Pocket sandwich (page 45) Banana 2 no-bake chocolate oatmeal cookies	Beef sandwich (made with leftovers from day 2 dinner) Carrot sticks Orange Crispy crunchy bar (page 62)
Snacks	2 pretzel rods Pear	Corn muffin Apple	2 pretzel rods Banana
Dinner	Tuna casserole (page 20) Sliced tomato on lettuce leaves 2 no-bake chocolate oatmeal cookies	Pot roast with vegetables (page 26) Biscuits (page 53) Strawberry shortcake (page 66)	Chow mein with noodles (page 6) Broccoli ($\frac{1}{2}$ 10-oz package) Fruity gelatin (page 63)

(continued)

Menu for Week B *(continued)*

DAY 4	DAY 5	DAY 6	DAY 7
Toaster waffles with syrup Orange	Toast with jelly Peach	Scrambled eggs (page 16) Sausage $\frac{1}{2}$ grapefruit	Fruit salad (page 31) English muffin Fruit juice
Beef sandwich Carrot sticks Banana Crispy crunchy bar	Tuna sandwich (page 48) Carrot sticks Orange Crispy crunchy bar	Cheeseburger (page 40) Sliced tomato on lettuce leaves Pudding parfait (page 65)	Chili (leftover from day 6) Celery sticks with salsa Pudding parfait
Crackers and peanut butter Apple	Corn Muffin Banana	English muffin Apple	2 pretzel rods Orange
Scalloped potatoes and ham (page 49) Broccoli ($\frac{1}{2}$ 10-oz package) Toast Fruity gelatin	Fish sticks Spanish rice (page 19) Tossed salad (page 36) Apple crisp (page 59)	Chili (page 5) Corn muffin Celery sticks with salsa Apple crisp	Spaghetti (page 18) Garlic roll (page 55) Tossed salad Apple crisp

Food Needs for Week A

(for 2 people)

Before shopping, check to see if you already have any of these items. Draw a line through the things you do not need to buy.

FRESH FRUITS AND VEGETABLES

1 head of lettuce

2 green peppers

$\frac{1}{4}$ head of cabbage

1 pound carrots

6 tomatoes

2 potatoes

1 onion

12 bananas

11 apples

9 oranges

1 grapefruit

1 peach

1 pear

MEAT

$2\frac{1}{4}$ pounds ground beef

6 hot dogs

4 chicken drumsticks

FROZEN FOODS

1 10-oz. package cut green beans

2 10-oz. packages mixed vegetables

DAIRY CASE

3 quarts milk

1 dozen eggs

2 quarts fruit juice

2 sticks margarine

8 slices cheese

1 package refrigerator crescent rolls

$\frac{1}{4}$ pound grated mozzarella cheese

1 cup ricotta cheese

whipped topping (such as Cool Whip®)

GRAINS/MIXES

crisp rice cereal (3 cups)

cereal (2 servings)

baking mix (such as Bisquick®) (3 cups)

instant rice (1 cup)

instant potato flakes ($\frac{3}{4}$ cup)

$\frac{1}{2}$ pound lasagna noodles

BAKERY

1 loaf bread

$\frac{1}{2}$ dozen English muffins

$\frac{1}{2}$ dozen sandwich rolls

$\frac{1}{2}$ dozen bagels

2 crusty rolls

CANNED FOODS

1 jar applesauce (16 oz.)

1 can tomatoes (8 oz.)

1 can baked beans (16 oz.)

1 can crushed pineapple (8 oz.)

1 can tomato sauce (8 oz.)

1 small can potato sticks

1 can cream of chicken soup

1 can chicken (5 oz.)

1 jar spaghetti sauce (16 oz.)

BAKING SUPPLIES

flour ($\frac{1}{4}$ cup)

sugar ($\frac{1}{2}$ cup)

cinnamon

garlic powder

parsley

oregano

cooking oil ($\frac{1}{4}$ cup)

instant chocolate pudding mix
  (6 servings)

instant vanilla pudding mix
  (4 servings)

BAKING SUPPLIES (continued)

prepared graham cracker crust

9 oz. yellow cake mix

chocolate chips ($\frac{1}{2}$ cup)

1 bag of marshmallows

paper muffin liners

OTHER

peanut butter

jelly

mayonnaise

salad dressing

vinegar

relish

mustard

ketchup

popcorn

grated Parmesan cheese

bacon bits (such as Bac-os®)

pancake syrup ($\frac{1}{4}$ cup)

What do you want to drink? Are there other special foods you want to buy?

_____

_____

_____

_____

_____

_____

_____

Food Needs for Week B

(for 2 people)

Before shopping, check to see if you already have any of these items. Draw a line through the things you do not need to buy.

FRESH FRUITS AND VEGETABLES

1 head of lettuce

1 green pepper

1 pound carrots

2 potatoes

4 tomatoes

1 cup bean sprouts

1 bunch celery

1 onion

$1\frac{1}{2}$ pints strawberries

9 oranges

3 peaches

1 grapefruit

10 apples

3 pears

10 bananas

MEAT

2 pork chops

$1\frac{3}{4}$ pounds ground beef

3- to $3\frac{1}{2}$-pound pot roast

3-oz. package corned beef

$\frac{1}{4}$ pound ham (thick-cut)

4 links sausage

FROZEN FOODS

1 package toaster waffles (8)

fish sticks (2 servings)

1 9-oz. package peas

1 10-oz. package broccoli

DAIRY CASE

2 quarts milk

$\frac{1}{2}$ dozen eggs

$1\frac{1}{2}$ quarts juice

3 sticks margarine

6 slices cheese

$\frac{1}{4}$ cup shredded cheese

whipped topping (such as Cool Whip®)

GRAINS/MIXES

crisp rice cereal (3 cups)

cereal (2 servings)

oatmeal (2 cups)

baking mix (like Bisquick®) (1 cup)

instant rice (1 cup)

spaghetti ($\frac{1}{2}$ 8-oz. package)

crackers

5-oz. box scalloped potato mix

7-oz box macaroni and cheese dinner

BAKERY

1 loaf bread

$\frac{1}{2}$ dozen English muffins

$\frac{1}{2}$ dozen corn muffins

2 hamburger rolls

1 9-inch pita round

2 crusty rolls

CANNED FOODS

1 can kidney beans (16 oz)

3 cans tomato sauce (8 oz.)

2 cans tuna (6 oz.)

1 can cream of mushroom soup

1 small can chow mein noodles

1 can apples (16 oz.)

1 can fruit cocktail (8 oz)

BAKING SUPPLIES

flour

sugar

brown sugar

cinnamon

cocoa

garlic powder

parsley

oregano

cooking oil

coconut

1 package gelatin dessert (such as Jell-O®) (4 servings)

1 package instant vanilla pudding mix (4 servings)

1 bag of marshmallows

pancake syrup

OTHER

peanut butter

jelly

mayonnaise

salad dressing

soy sauce

cornstarch

salsa

relish

mustard

1 envelope onion soup mix

1 envelope chili seasoning mix

1 small bag potato chips

1 bag pretzel rods

1 jar pickles

What do you want to drink? Are there other special foods you want to buy?

_____

_____

_____

_____

_____

_____

_____

_____

_____

_____

_____

PART 1

Main Dishes

Chicken Noodle Casserole

Preheat Oven to 350°

Cook Noodles

Ingredients:

½ 8-oz. package egg noodles

Utensils:

saucepan with cover

Directions:

1. Half fill saucepan with water.
2. Cover; bring to a boil over high heat.
3. Add noodles.
4. Bring to a boil again.
5. Stir noodles; cover; turn heat to low.
6. Cook 6 to 8 minutes.
7. Drain.

Mix Casserole

Ingredients:

1 can cream of chicken soup

⅓ cup milk

½ 10-oz. package frozen cut green beans

1 5-oz. can chicken

1 small can french-fried onion rings

Utensils:

small casserole dish

can opener

measuring cup

mixing spoon

Directions:

8. Open can of soup and empty into casserole dish.
9. Measure milk; add to casserole; mix well.
10. Add beans to casserole.
11. Open can of chicken; add to casserole.
12. Add noodles to casserole.
13. Add half the can of onions to the casserole.
14. Mix ingredients well.
15. Bake uncovered 30 minutes.
16. Top with rest of onions.
17. Bake 5 minutes more.

Preheat Oven to 400°

2 servings

Prepare Filling

Ingredients:	Utensils:	Directions:
1 9-oz. package mixed frozen vegetables 1 can cream of chicken soup 1 5-oz. can chicken	saucepan with cover wooden spoon can opener	1. Put 1 inch of water in bottom of saucepan. 2. Add vegetables to pan. 3. Bring to a boil. 4. Stir gently. 5. Cover pan and simmer 7 to 10 minutes or until vegetables are tender. 6. Drain water from vegetables. 7. Open can of soup; add to vegetables. 8. Open can of chicken; add to vegetables; stir gently.

Bake Pie

Ingredients:	Utensils:	Directions:
4 refrigerator crescent rolls	loaf pan	9. Pour filling into loaf pan. 10. Arrange crescent roll dough to cover filling. 11. Bake 12 to 15 minutes or until crust is browned.

Chili

Prepare Meat

Ingredients:	*Utensils:*	*Directions:*
1 pound ground beef	skillet wooden spoon	1. Put ground beef in skillet; cook over medium heat until browned.

Add Remaining Ingredients

Ingredients:	*Utensils:*	*Directions:*
1 16-oz. can kidney beans 2 8-oz. cans tomato sauce $\frac{1}{2}$ cup water 1 package chili seasoning mix	can opener measuring cup	2. Open can of beans; add to skillet. 3. Open cans of tomato sauce; add to skillet. 4. Measure water into skillet. 5. Open package of seasoning mix; add to skillet. 6. Stir mixture. 7. Bring mixture to a boil. 8. Turn heat to low; simmer 15 minutes.

Cook Meat

Ingredients:	Utensils:	Directions:
2 pork chops	paring knife skillet with cover wooden spoon	1. Remove bones from meat. 2. Cut pork into thin strips. 3. Heat pan over medium-high heat. 4. Cook meat; stir until no pink remains; if meat sticks to the skillet, add a little margarine.

Cook Vegetables

Ingredients:	Utensils:	Directions:
1 small onion 4 stalks celery 1 cup water 1 cup bean sprouts	cutting board measuring cup	5. Peel onion; chop; add to skillet. 6. Trim brown spots from celery; chop; add to skillet. 7. Measure 1 cup water into skillet. *(continued)*

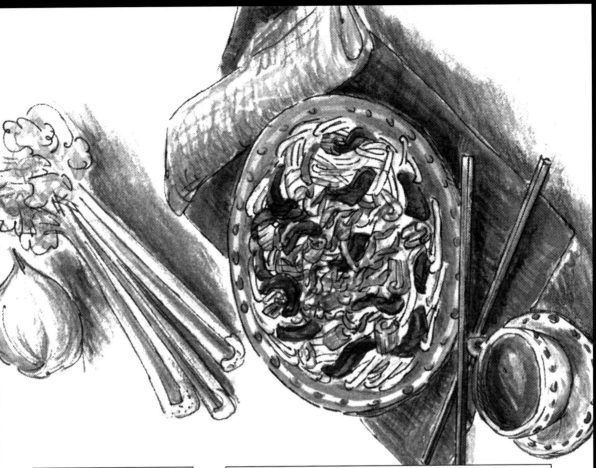

Cook Vegetables *(continued)*

	Directions:
	8. Cover; cook over medium heat 8 to 10 minutes until vegetables are cooked.
	9. Add bean sprouts to skillet.

Make Sauce

Ingredients:	*Utensils:*	*Directions:*
2 tablespoons soy sauce	measuring spoon	10. Measure soy sauce into bowl.
1 tablespoon cornstarch	small bowl	11. Measure cornstarch into bowl.
1 tablespoon brown sugar	mixing spoon	12. Measure brown sugar into bowl.
1 small can chow mein noodles		13. Mix ingredients in small bowl; add to skillet.
		14. Cook until mixture thickens.
		15. Serve topped with chow mein noodles.

Cook Vegetables

Ingredients:	Utensils:	Directions:
1 tablespoon margarine 1 small onion $\frac{1}{2}$ cup water 1 1-pound can potatoes	saucepan paring knife cutting board wooden spoon measuring cup can opener fork	1. Put margarine in saucepan; melt over medium heat. 2. Peel onion; chop; add to saucepan. 3. Stir and cook until onion is soft. 4. Measure $\frac{1}{2}$ cup water into saucepan. 5. Open can of potatoes; slice potatoes and add to saucepan. 6. Cook 10 minutes; test potatoes with a fork to be sure they are soft.

Finish Chowder

Ingredients:		Directions:
1 1-pound can cream-style corn 2 cups		7. Open corn; add to saucepan. 8. Measure milk into saucepan. 9. Heat over medium heat until warmed through; do not boil.

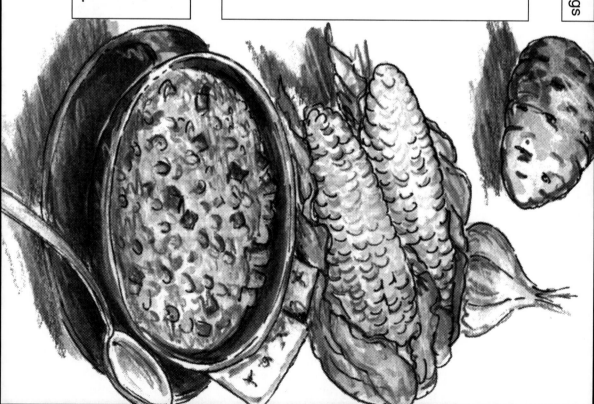

French Toast

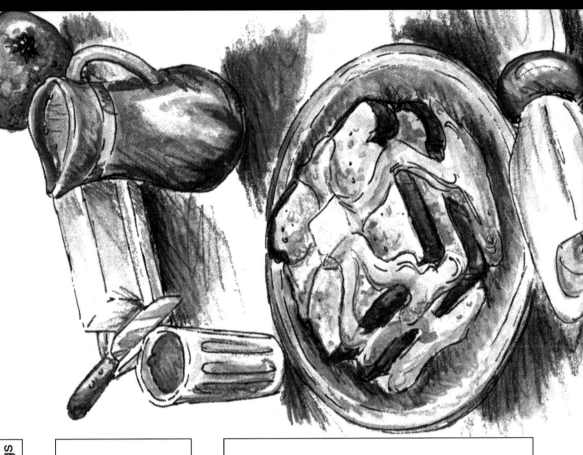

Prepare Egg Mixture

Ingredients:	*Utensils:*	*Directions:*
1 egg	shallow soup bowl	1. Break egg into bowl.
$\frac{1}{4}$ cup milk	measuring cup	2. Measure milk into bowl.
	fork	3. Use fork to mix egg and milk together.

Cook French Toast

Ingredients:	*Utensils:*	*Directions:*
$\frac{1}{2}$ teaspoon cooking oil	skillet	4. Heat skillet over medium heat.
2 slices bread	spatula	5. Grease skillet with cooking oil.
pancake syrup		6. Dip bread, one slice at a time, into the egg mixture.
		7. Cook one side about 4 minutes or until golden brown.
		8. Turn with spatula and cook other side about 4 minutes.
		9. Serve with syrup.

4 servings

Preheat Oven to 350°

Prepare Cheese

Ingredients:	Utensils:	Directions:
1 cup ricotta cheese	small bowl	1. Measure cheese into bowl.
1 egg	measuring cup	2. Break egg into bowl.
	mixing spoon	3. Mix together.

Cook Lasagna Noodles

Ingredients:	Utensils:	Directions:
$\frac{1}{2}$ pound lasagna noodles	saucepan	4. Half fill saucepan with water; boil.
		5. Add lasagna, one noodle at a time; as each noodle softens and fits in pan, add next.
		6. Cook about 9 minutes.
		7. Drain water.
		8. Rinse noodles in cold water; drain water.

(continued)

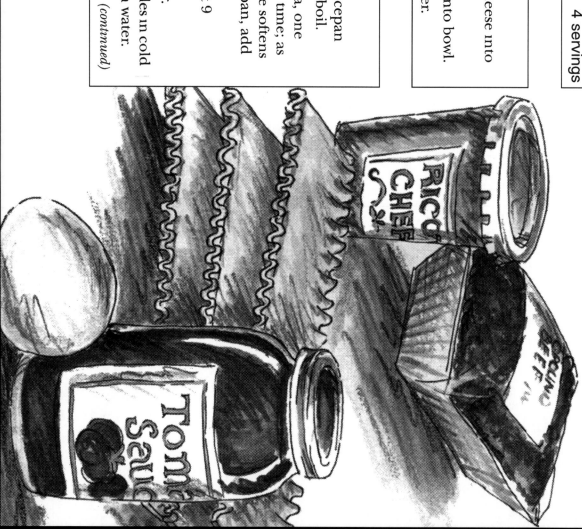

10

Prepare Sauce

Ingredients:	Utensils:	Directions:
$\frac{1}{2}$ pound ground beef	skillet	9. Put ground beef into skillet; cook over medium heat.
1 16-oz. jar spaghetti sauce	wooden spoon	10. Add spaghetti sauce to pan.
	square baking dish	11. Mix together.
		12. Place a layer of noodles in bottom of the pan; cut noodles as needed.
		13. Spread one half the cheese on the noodles.
		14. Spread one third of the sauce over the cheese.
		15. Repeat steps 12, 13, & 14.
		16. Add a last layer of noodles.
		17 Top with remaining sauce.
		18. Bake 30 minutes.
		19. Let stand 10 minutes before serving.

Make Batter

Ingredients:

2 cups baking mix (such as Bisquick®)

$1\frac{1}{4}$ cups milk

2 eggs

Utensils:

mixing bowl

measuring cup

mixing spoon

Directions:

1. Measure baking mix into bowl.
2. Add milk.
3. Add eggs.
4. Mix all ingredients together.

Cook Pancakes

Ingredients:

$\frac{1}{2}$ teaspoon oil

Utensils:

skillet

measuring cup

Directions:

5. Heat skillet over medium heat.
6. Cover surface of pan with oil.
7. Fill measuring cup with batter.
8. Pour batter from measuring cup onto hot skillet; use about $\frac{1}{4}$ cup batter for each pancake.
9. Let pancakes get full of bubbles.
10. Turn pancakes and brown on second side.
11. Cook rest of batter by repeating steps 7–10.

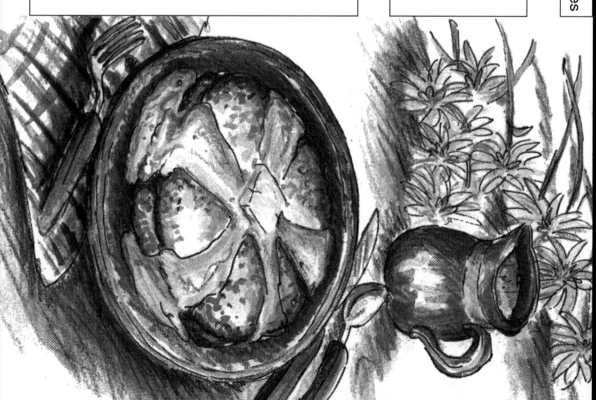

Pigs in a Blanket

Preheat Oven to 350°

2 servings

Wrap Hot Dogs

Ingredients:	*Utensils:*	*Directions:*
4 refrigerator crescent rolls 4 hot dogs	baking sheet	1. Place triangle of dough on baking sheet. 2. Place hot dog on wide end of dough. 3. Roll dough around hot dog. 4. Repeat for other 3 rolls.

Bake Hot Dogs

Ingredients:		*Directions:*
mustard relish		5. Bake 10 to 14 minutes or until dough is browned. 6. Serve with mustard and relish.

Prepare Beans

Ingredients:	Utensils:	Directions:
1 16-oz. can baked beans	can opener	1. Open can of beans; empty into saucepan.
1 8-oz. can crushed pineapple	saucepan measuring cup wooden spoon	2. Open can of pineapple; add to saucepan.
$\frac{1}{4}$ cup ketchup		3. Measure ketchup into saucepan.
		4. Mix together.

Add Franks

Ingredients:	Utensils:	Directions:
2 hot dogs	paring knife cutting board	5. Cut hot dogs into $\frac{1}{2}$-inch slices.
		6. Add hot dogs to saucepan.
		7. Heat over medium heat until bubbly.

Scalloped Potatoes and Ham

Preheat Oven to 400°

Mix Casserole

Ingredients:	*Utensils:*	*Directions:*
1 5-oz. box scalloped potato mix	small casserole dish	1. Open box of potatoes and empty into casserole dish.
$2\frac{1}{3}$ cups boiling water	measuring cup	2. Measure boiling water into dish.
$\frac{2}{3}$ cup milk	sharp knife	3. Measure milk into dish.
$\frac{1}{2}$ 9-oz. package frozen green peas	cutting board	4. Measure peas into dish.
$\frac{1}{4}$ pound thick-cut ham	mixing spoon	5. Cut ham into small pieces; add to dish.
		6. Mix ingredients.

Bake Casserole

Utensils:	*Directions:*
fork	7. Bake uncovered in oven about 35 minutes; test potatoes with a fork to be sure they are tender.

15

Mix Eggs

Ingredients:

4 eggs

2 tablespoons water

Utensils:

small bowl

measuring spoons

fork

Directions:

1. Break eggs into bowl.
2. Add water to eggs.
3. Mix with fork.

Cook Eggs

Ingredients:

$\frac{1}{2}$ teaspoon margarine

Utensils:

skillet

spatula

Directions:

4. Put margarine in skillet.
5. Melt over medium heat.
6. Pour egg mixture into skillet.
7. Cook 3 to 5 minutes.
8. While cooking, stir once or twice with spatula.
9. Eggs should be thick, but still moist.

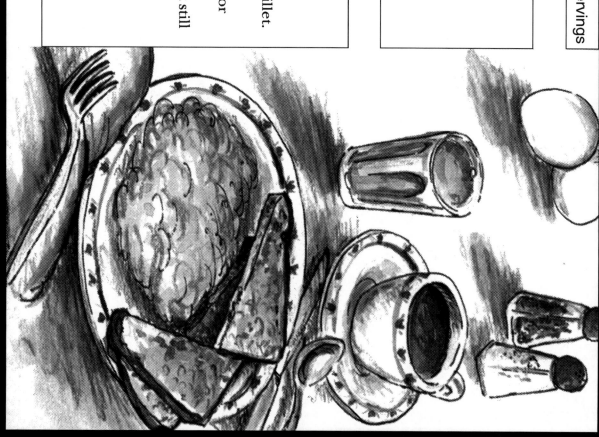

Shepherd's Pie

2 servings

Preheat Oven to 350°

Prepare Potatoes

Ingredients:	Utensils:	Directions:
$\frac{2}{3}$ cup water	saucepan	1. Measure water into saucepan; heat to boiling.
$\frac{1}{4}$ cup milk	measuring cup	2. Remove pan from heat.
$\frac{2}{3}$ cup potato flakes	wooden spoon	3. Measure milk into saucepan.
		4. Measure potato flakes into saucepan; stir; let stand until liquid is absorbed.

Prepare Meat

Ingredients:	Utensils:	Directions:
$\frac{1}{2}$ pound ground beef	skillet	5. Brown ground beef in skillet.
$\frac{1}{2}$ 12-oz. can gravy		6. Add gravy; mix together.

Assemble Casserole

Ingredients:	Utensils:	Directions:
1 8-oz. can whole-kernel corn	loaf pan	7. Spread meat mixture in bottom of loaf pan.
	can opener	8. Open can of corn; drain liquid; spread corn over meat mixture.
		9. Spoon potatoes onto corn.
		10. Bake 30 minutes or until potatoes begin to brown.

Prepare Sauce

Ingredients:	Utensils:	Directions:
$\frac{1}{4}$ pound ground beef	saucepan	1. Brown beef over low heat; stir constantly.
1 8-oz. can tomato sauce	wooden spoon	2. Open can of tomato sauce; add to pan.
1 teaspoon oregano	can opener	3. Measure oregano into saucepan.
	measuring spoons	4. Mix ingredients together.
		5. Simmer over low heat.

Cook Spaghetti

Ingredients:	Utensils:	Directions:
$\frac{1}{2}$ 8-oz. package of spaghetti	saucepan with cover	6. Half fill the saucepan with water.
		7. Cover and bring to a boil over high heat.
		8. Add spaghetti.
		9. Bring to a boil again.
		10. Stir spaghetti; cover; reduce heat to low.
		11. Cook 15 minutes.
		12. Drain.
		13. Serve with sauce.

Spanish Rice

Cook Rice

Ingredients:

1 cup water

$\frac{1}{4}$ teaspoon salt

1 cup instant rice

Utensils:

saucepan with cover

wooden spoon

Directions:

1. Measure water and salt into saucepan.

2. Cover and bring to a boil over high heat.

3. Measure rice into boiling water; stir.

4. Remove from heat; let stand 5 minutes or until the water is absorbed.

Prepare Sauce

Ingredients:

$\frac{1}{4}$ pound ground beef

8-oz. can tomatoes

$\frac{1}{2}$ teaspoon parsley

Utensils:

skillet

can opener

measuring spoons

Directions:

5. Put ground beef into skillet; cook over medium heat until browned.

6. Open can of tomatoes; add to skillet.

7. Measure parsley into skillet.

8. Simmer sauce over medium heat.

9. Add cooked rice to skillet.

10. Cook uncovered over low heat for 10 minutes.

19

Tuna Casserole

Preheat Oven to 350°

Cook Macaroni

Ingredients:	Utensils:	Directions:
1 7-oz. package macaroni & cheese dinner	saucepan with cover wooden spoon	1. Half fill saucepan with water; cover and bring to a boil over high heat. 2. Add macaroni to boiling water; bring to a boil again. 3. Stir; cover; turn heat to low. 4. Cook 8 to 10 minutes. 5. Drain macaroni.

Mix Casserole

Ingredients:	Utensils:	Directions:
$\frac{1}{4}$ stick margarine $\frac{1}{4}$ cup milk 1 6-oz. can tuna 1 $\frac{1}{2}$ 9-oz. package frozen green peas 1 small bag potato chips	measuring cup can opener small casserole	6. Add margarine to hot macaroni. 7. Measure milk and add to saucepan. 8. Empty contents of cheese package into saucepan. 9. Stir ingredients. 10. Open can of tuna; add to macaroni mixture. 11. Add peas. 12. Mix gently. 13. Spoon mixture into casserole dish. 14. Crush potato chips; sprinkle crumbs over casserole. 15. Bake 25 to 30 minutes.

PART 2

Meat and Chicken

Meat Loaf

Preheat Oven to 350°

6 servings

Mix Ingredients

Ingredients:	Utensils:	Directions:
1½ pounds ground beef 2 slices bread ½ cup milk 1 egg 1 small onion	mixing bowl measuring cup paring knife cutting board	1. Put ground beef in bowl. 2. Tear bread into small pieces; add to bowl. 3. Measure milk; add to bowl. 4. Break egg into bowl. 5. Peel onion; chop; add to bowl. 6. Mix all ingredients together.

Cook the Meat Loaf

Utensils:	Directions:
loaf pan spatula plate	7. Place mixture in loaf pan; press down firmly. 8. Bake 1 hour. 9. Use spatula to lift meat out of pan and put on plate.

Prepare Sauce

Ingredients:	Utensils:	Directions:
2 teaspoons cornstarch $\frac{1}{2}$ teaspoon sugar $\frac{1}{2}$ cup cold water 1 tablespoon soy sauce	measuring cup measuring spoons small bowl mixing spoon	1. Measure cornstarch into bowl. 2. Measure sugar into bowl. 3. Measure cold water; slowly pour into bowl while mixing ingredients together. 4. Measure soy sauce into bowl; mix together.

Cook Meat and Vegetables

Ingredients:	Utensils:	Directions:
1 green pepper $\frac{1}{2}$ pound chuck steak 1 tablespoon cooking oil	paring knife cutting board sharp knife skillet wooden spoon	5. Remove seeds from green pepper; cut pepper into strips. 6. Cut steak into 2 pieces. 7. Heat skillet over medium-high heat. 8. Cook steak until browned on one side; turn and cook other side; remove from skillet; if steak starts to stick to the skillet, add a little margarine. 9. Measure oil into skillet. 10. Add green pepper to skillet; stir and cook until softened. 11. Add sauce; stir until thick and bubbly. 12. Spoon over steaks.

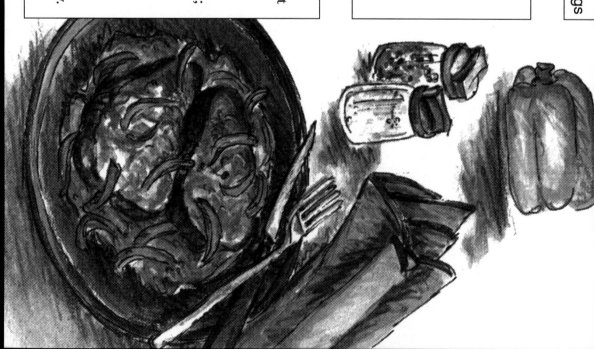

Oven-Fried Chicken

Preheat Oven to 400°

2 servings

Prepare the Chicken

Ingredients:	Utensils:	Directions:
2 tablespoons flour	plastic bag	1. Measure flour into plastic bag.
4 chicken drumsticks	measuring spoons	2. Put a drumstick into the bag and coat with flour.
		3. Repeat with remaining chicken pieces.

Cook the Chicken

Ingredients:	Utensils:	Directions:
2 tablespoons margarine	loaf pan	4. Put margarine in loaf pan.
	fork	5. Put pan in oven and melt margarine.
		6. Remove pan from oven; turn chicken pieces in melted margarine until coated.
		7. Arrange chicken in pan skin side down.
		8. Bake 20 minutes.
		9. Lower heat to 350°.
		10. Turn chicken skin side up.
		11. Bake 15 to 20 minutes more.

Cook Meat

Ingredients:	Utensils:	Directions:
1 tablespoon cooking oil	soup kettle with cover	1. Measure oil and pour into kettle; place kettle over medium heat.
3- to 3½-pound pot roast	measuring spoons	2. Brown roast on all sides.
1 can cream of mushroom soup	wooden spoon	3. Open mushroom soup; empty into bowl.
1 envelope onion soup mix	can opener	4. Empty envelope of onion soup mix into bowl.
	small bowl	5. Measure water; gradually add to bowl while stirring.
	measuring cup	6. Pour soup mixture into kettle.
		7. Cover kettle.
		8. Turn heat to low; simmer 3 to 3½ hours.

Add Vegetables

Ingredients:	Utensils:	Directions:
potatoes (1 for each person)	paring knife	9. After meat has cooked 2 to 2½ hours, add vegetables.
carrots (2 for each person)	cutting board	10. Wash potatoes; cut into quarters; add to kettle.
	vegetable peeler	11. Peel carrots; cut into 2-inch pieces; add to kettle.
	fork	12. Keep kettle covered and cook until vegetables are soft.

PART 3

Vegetables and Salads

Cheesy Potato Puffs

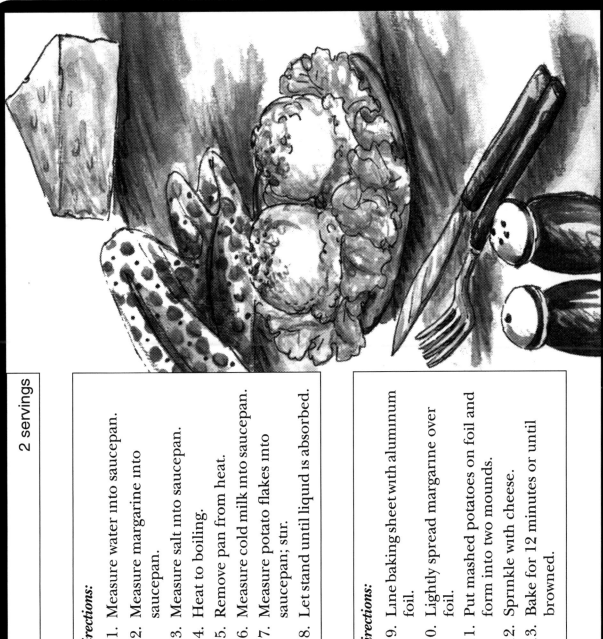

2 servings

Preheat Oven to 450°

Make Mashed Potatoes

Ingredients:	Utensils:	Directions:
$\frac{2}{3}$ cup water	saucepan	1. Measure water into saucepan.
1 tablespoon margarine	measuring cup	2. Measure margarine into saucepan.
$\frac{1}{4}$ teaspoon salt	measuring spoons	3. Measure salt into saucepan.
$\frac{1}{4}$ cup milk	wooden spoon	4. Heat to boiling.
$\frac{3}{4}$ cup instant potato flakes		5. Remove pan from heat.
		6. Measure cold milk into saucepan.
		7. Measure potato flakes into saucepan; stir.
		8. Let stand until liquid is absorbed.

Bake Potato Puffs

Ingredients:	Utensils:	Directions:
$\frac{1}{2}$ teaspoon margarine	baking sheet	9. Line baking sheet with aluminum foil.
2 teaspoons grated Parmesan cheese	aluminum foil	10. Lightly spread margarine over foil.
		11. Put mashed potatoes on foil and form into two mounds.
		12. Sprinkle with cheese.
		13. Bake for 12 minutes or until browned.

29

2 servings

Prepare Vegetables

Ingredients:	Utensils:	Directions:
$\frac{1}{4}$ small cabbage 1 carrot	vegetable grater mixing bowl vegetable peeler	1. Remove outer leaves of cabbage. 2. Grate cabbage into bowl. 3. Peel carrot. 4. Grate carrot into bowl.

Prepare Dressing

Ingredients:	Utensils:	Directions:
2 tablespoons mayonnaise 1 tablespoon vinegar 1 teaspoon sugar	small bowl measuring spoons mixing spoon	5. Measure mayonnaise into small bowl. 6. Measure vinegar into small bowl. 7. Measure sugar into small bowl. 8. Mix dressing. 9. Add dressing to vegetables; mix well.

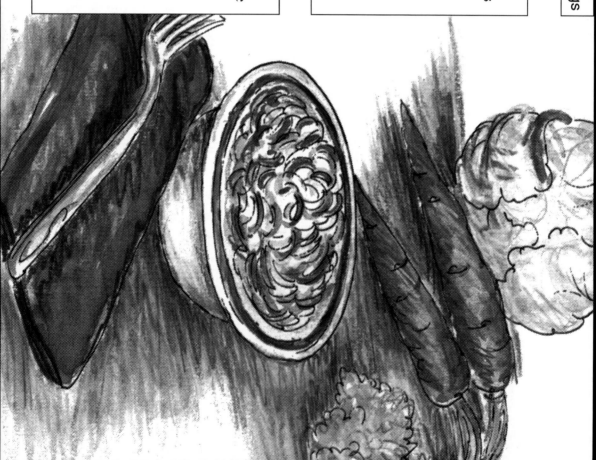

Fruit Salad

Prepare Fruit

Ingredients:

1 orange
1 apple
1 banana
1 peach
1 pear

Utensils:

mixing or
  serving bowl
paring knife
cutting board

Directions:

1. Peel orange; break into sections; cut each section in half; put in bowl.

2. Cut apple into 4 pieces; remove core; chop; add to bowl.

3. Peel banana; slice; add to bowl.

4. Peel peach; cut in half; remove pit; cut peach into small pieces; add to bowl.

5. Cut pear into 4 pieces; remove core; chop; add to bowl.

Finish Salad

Utensils:

mixing spoon

Directions:

6. Mix fruit together.

7. Keep salad in refrigerator until serving time.

Cook Potatoes

Ingredients:	Utensils:	Directions:
3 medium potatoes	saucepan with cover fork	1. Wash potatoes. 2. Put potatoes in saucepan. 3. Cover potatoes with water. 4. Put cover on pan. 5. Heat to boiling; cook 25 minutes or until fork goes into potatoes easily. 6. Remove potatoes from water; cool.

Prepare Vegetables

Ingredients:	Utensils:	Directions:
1 small onion ½ green pepper	medium bowl paring knife cutting board	7. Cut potatoes into cubes (no need to peel); put in bowl. 8. Peel onion; chop; add to bowl. 9. Remove seeds from pepper; chop; add to bowl.

(continued)

Potato Salad *(continued)*

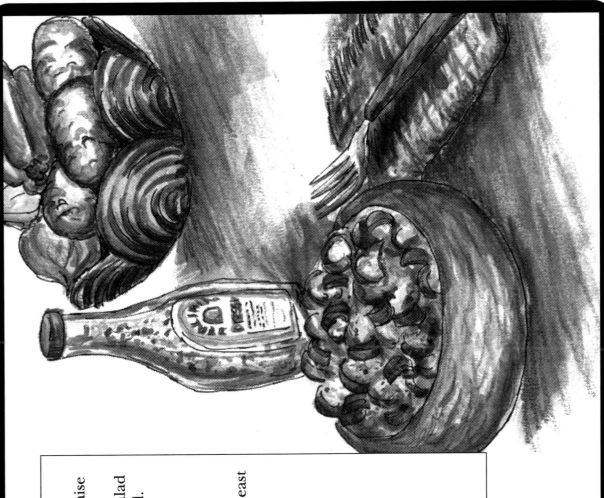

Add Dressing

Ingredients:

¼ cup
mayonnaise

2 tablespoons
Italian salad
dressing

Utensils:

small bowl

measuring cup

measuring
spoons

Directions:

10. Measure mayonnaise
    into small bowl.

11. Measure Italian salad
    dressing into bowl.

12. Mix ingredients.

13. Add dressing to
    vegetables; mix
    together.

14. Refrigerate for at least
    2 hours before
    serving.

Preheat Oven to 350°

2 servings

Mix Casserole

Ingredients:	Utensils:	Directions:
1 8-oz. can cream-style corn 8 saltine crackers $\frac{1}{4}$ cup milk 1 egg	small oven-proof bowl can opener measuring cup mixing spoon	1. Open corn; empty into bowl. 2. Break crackers into fine crumbs; add to bowl. 3. Measure milk into bowl. 4. Break egg into bowl. 5. Mix ingredients together.

Bake Corn

Ingredients:		Directions:
$\frac{3}{4}$ cup croutons		6. Sprinkle croutons over corn mixture. 7. Bake 35–40 minutes.

Stuffed Baked Potatoes

2 servings

Preheat Oven to 350°

Bake Potatoes

Ingredients:	*Utensils:*	*Directions:*
2 medium potatoes	fork	1. Wash potatoes.
		2. Use fork to pierce potatoes several times.
		3. Bake potatoes 1 hour or until fork goes easily into the potatoes.

Prepare Topping

Ingredients:	*Utensils:*	*Directions:*
$\frac{1}{2}$ cup ricotta cheese	sharp knife	4. Cut a deep cross in the top of each potato.
2 tablespoons bacon bits (like Bac-os®)	serving spoon	5. Spoon cheese on top of each potato.
		6. Sprinkle bacon bits on each potato.

Prepare Vegetables

Ingredients:	*Utensils:*	*Directions:*
$\frac{1}{4}$ head lettuce	salad bowl	1. Remove core from lettuce.
1 tomato	paring knife	2. Wash lettuce leaves.
1 carrot	chopping board	3. Tear lettuce leaves into small pieces; place in bowl.
$\frac{1}{4}$ green pepper	vegetable peeler	4. Remove core from tomato; cut into wedges; add to bowl.
		5. Peel carrot; slice; add to bowl.
		6. Remove seeds from pepper; chop; add to bowl.

Serve the Salad

Ingredients:	*Utensils:*	*Directions:*
4 tablespoons salad dressing	measuring spoons	7. Pour salad dressing over vegetables just before serving.
	large fork and spoon	8. Toss lightly with fork and spoon.

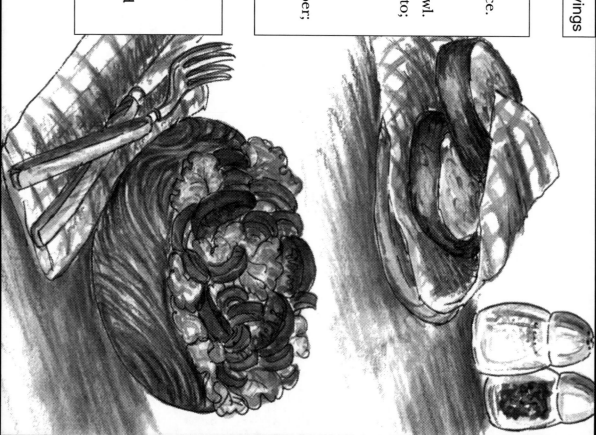

PART 4

Sandwiches

BLT Sandwiches

(Bacon, Lettuce, and Tomato)

2 sandwiches

Cook Bacon

Ingredients:	*Utensils:*	*Directions:*
8 slices bacon	skillet fork paper towels	1. Put bacon in skillet; cook over medium heat. 2. Turn often and cook 4 or 5 minutes until crisp. 3. Place paper towels on counter; put cooked bacon on paper towels to drain.

Make Sandwiches

Ingredients:	*Utensils:*	*Directions:*
4 slices bread 2 tablespoons mayonnause 4 lettuce leaves 1 tomato	butter knife paring knife cutting board	4. Spread mayonnause on 2 slices of bread. 5. Place lettuce leaves on bread with mayonnause. 6. Remove core from tomato; slice tomato; place slices on lettuce. 7. Place bacon on tomato. 8. Top with other 2 slices of bread.

Cook Hamburgers

Ingredients:	Utensils:	Directions:
$\frac{1}{2}$ pound ground beef 2 slices cheese	skillet spatula	1. Shape meat into 2 patties. 2. Heat skillet over medium-high heat. 3. Put hamburger patties in skillet. 4. Cook 3 to 4 minutes. 5. Turn patties. 6. Top each patty with a slice of cheese. 7. Continue cooking until meat is done and cheese melts.

Serve Cheeseburgers

Ingredients:		Directions:
2 hamburger rolls mustard relish		8. Place hamburger patties in rolls. 9. Serve with mustard and relish.

Egg Salad Sandwiches

Cook Hard-Boiled Eggs

Ingredients:	Utensils:	Directions:
2 eggs	saucepan with cover	1. Put eggs in saucepan.
		2. Cover eggs with water.
		3. Heat on high to boiling.
		4. Cover pan; remove from heat; let stand 20 minutes.
		5. Drain hot water.
		6. Rinse eggs with cold water.

Make Salad

Ingredients:	Utensils:	Directions:
$1\frac{1}{2}$ tablespoons mayonnaise	small bowl	7. Tap eggs to crack shells.
$\frac{1}{2}$ teaspoon parsley	fork	8. Roll eggs on counter to loosen shell; peel eggs.
dash pepper	measuring spoon	9. Rinse eggs to remove pieces of shell.
4 slices bread		10. Put eggs in bowl; mash with a fork.
		11. Measure mayonnaise into bowl.
		12. Measure parsley into bowl; add pepper.
		13. Mix ingredients together.
		14. Spread salad on bread to make 2 sandwiches.

2 sandwiches

Prepare Sandwiches

Ingredients:
4 slices bread
4 slices cheese

Directions:
1. Place 2 slices of cheese on 2 slices of bread.
2. Top with remaining bread.

Grill Sandwiches

Ingredients:
2 tablespoons softened margarine

Utensils:
butter knife
skillet
spatula

Directions:
3. Spread half of margarine on one side of both sandwiches.
4. Heat skillet over medium heat.
5. Place sandwiches in heated skillet, margarine side down.
6. Spread remaining margarine on sides facing up.
7. When first side is golden brown, turn and grill on second side.

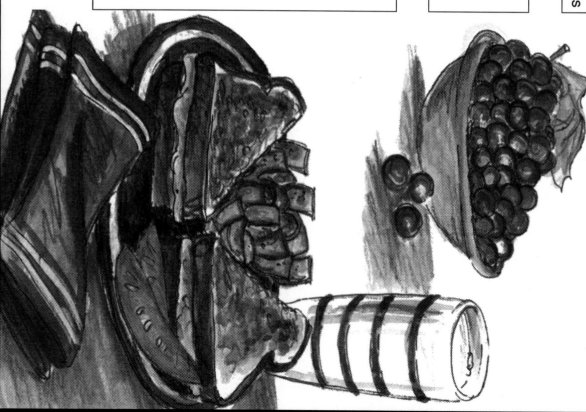

Open-Faced Turkey Sandwiches

Heat Gravy

Ingredients:	Utensils:	Directions:
$\frac{1}{2}$ 12-oz. jar turkey gravy	small saucepan wooden spoon	1. Pour half the jar of gravy into the saucepan. 2. Heat over medium heat until bubbly. 3. Stir to keep from burning gravy.

Make Sandwiches

Ingredients:	Utensils:	Directions:
4 slices bread 4 slices turkey	2 lunch plates	4. Toast the bread. 5. Place 2 slices of toast on each plate. 6. Put a slice of turkey on each piece of toast. 7. Pour gravy over the turkey.

43

Preheat Oven to 425°

2 servings

Prepare Bagels

Ingredients:	Utensils:	Directions:
2 plain bagels	sharp knife	1. Cut bagels in half.
	toaster	2. Toast bagels.
	baking sheet	3. Put toasted bagels on baking sheet.

Assemble Pizzas

Ingredients:	Utensils:	Directions:
1 8-oz. can tomato sauce	can opener	4. Open sauce and pour into bowl.
$\frac{1}{2}$ teaspoon oregano	small bowl	5. Measure oregano into bowl.
$\frac{1}{4}$ pound grated mozzarella cheese	measuring spoons	6. Mix together.
	mixing spoon	7. Spoon sauce onto bagels.
		8. Sprinkle bagels with cheese.
		9. Heat in oven 10 to 15 minutes until cheese melts.

Pocket Sandwiches

Prepare Bread

Ingredients:	Utensils:	Directions:
1 9-inch pita round	bread knife	1. Cut pita round in half.
2 tablespoons mustard	butter knife	2. Open both halves of the bread to make pockets.
		3. Spread mustard inside each pocket.

Add the Filling

Ingredients:		Directions:
1 3-oz. package corned beef		4. Arrange half of the corned beef in each pocket.
4 lettuce leaves		5. Add 2 lettuce leaves to each pocket.
$\frac{1}{4}$ cup shredded cheese		6. Add shredded cheese to each pocket.
10 pickle slices		7. Add pickle slices to each pocket.

Sloppy Joes

2 servings

Prepare Filling

Ingredients:	Utensils:	Directions:
$\frac{1}{2}$ pound ground beef 1 8-oz. can tomato sauce $\frac{1}{4}$ cup ketchup	skillet wooden spoon can opener measuring cup	1. Put ground beef in skillet; cook over medium heat until browned; drain fat. 2. Open tomato sauce; add to skillet. 3. Measure ketchup into skillet. 4. Mix ingredients together. 5. Heat until bubbly.

Serve

Ingredients:	Utensils:	Directions:
2 hamburger rolls	2 lunch plates	6. Open hamburger rolls. 7. Place an opened roll on each plate. 8. Spoon filling over rolls.

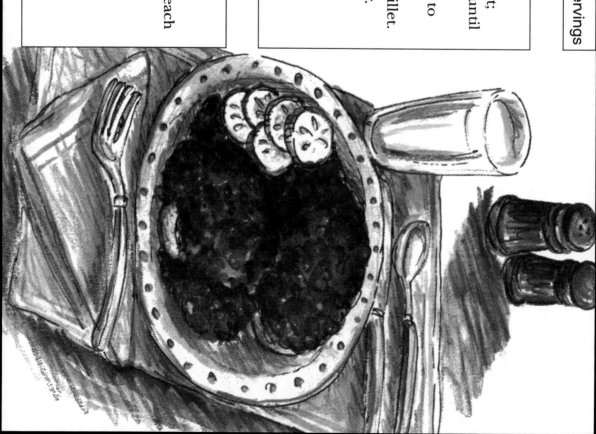

46

Tacos

Preheat Oven to 350°

6 tacos

Make Meat Filling

Ingredients:	Utensils:	Directions:
$\frac{1}{2}$ pound ground beef $\frac{1}{2}$ envelope taco seasoning mix $\frac{1}{2}$ cup water	skillet wooden spoon measuring cup	1. Put ground beef in skillet; cook over medium heat; drain fat. 2. Add seasoning mix to the skillet. 3. Measure water into the skillet. 4. Bring to a boil; turn down heat and simmer 10 to 15 minutes.

Heat Shells

Ingredients:	Utensils:	Directions:
6 taco shells	baking sheet	5. Place shells on baking sheet. 6. Put 1 to 2 tablespoons meat filling in each shell. 7. Bake 5 to 7 minutes.

Finish Tacos

Ingredients:	Utensils:	Directions:
2 tomatoes $\frac{1}{4}$ head lettuce 1 cup shredded cheese	paring knife chopping board	8. Remove cores from tomatoes; chop. 9. Remove core from lettuce; chop. 10. Add tomato, lettuce, and cheese to each taco.

47

Prepare Filling

Ingredients:	Utensils:	Directions:
1 6-oz. can tuna	can opener	1. Open can of tuna and drain liquid.
1 tablespoon relish	small bowl	2. Place tuna in small bowl.
1 tablespoon mayonnaise	fork	3. Use fork to break up the fish.
	measuring spoon	4. Measure relish into the bowl.
		5. Measure mayonnaise into the bowl.
		6. Mix ingredients together.

Make Sandwiches

Ingredients:		Directions:
4 slices bread		7. Spread filling on 2 slices of bread.
4 leaves lettuce		8. Add 2 leaves of lettuce.
		9. Cover with remaining bread.

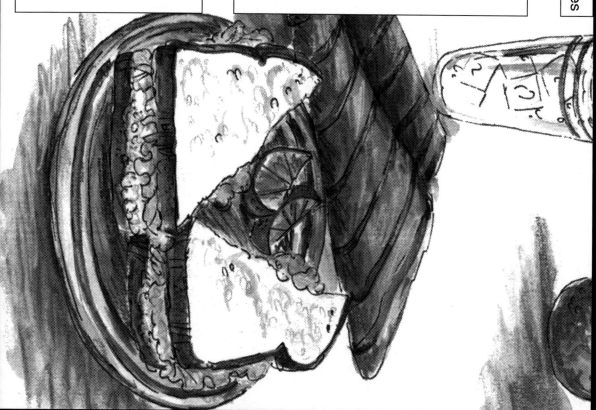

Veggie Hero Sandwiches

2 sandwiches

Prepare Bread

Ingredients:	Utensils:	Directions:
2 sandwich rolls 2 tablespoons mayonnaise	bread knife butter knife	1. Cut rolls open. 2. Spread inside of rolls with mayonnaise.

Chop Vegetables

Ingredients:	Utensils:	Directions:
2 large leaves of lettuce $\frac{1}{2}$ green pepper 1 tomato	paring knife cutting board	3. Chop lettuce. 4. Remove seeds from pepper; chop. 5. Remove tomato core; cut into wedges.

Put Sandwiches Together

Ingredients:		Directions:
4 slices cheese salt pepper		6. Put in each roll: • 2 slices cheese • lettuce • green pepper • tomato wedges 7. Sprinkle with salt and pepper.

49

PART 5

Breads

Biscuits

Preheat Oven to 450°

4 biscuits

Prepare Dough

Ingredients:	Utensils:	Directions:
1 cup baking mix (such as Bisquick®) $\frac{1}{3}$ cup milk	measuring cup mixing bowl mixing spoon	1. Measure baking mix into bowl. 2. Measure milk into bowl. 3. Mix together.

Bake Biscuits

Ingredients:	Utensils:	Directions:
flour $\frac{1}{2}$ teaspoon margarine	knife baking sheet	4. Sprinkle 2 or 3 tablespoons of flour on counter. 5. Put dough on flour. 6. Roll dough to cover with flour; knead 3 or 4 times. 7. Shape into square 6 inches by 6 inches. 8. Cut into 4 square biscuits. 9. Grease baking sheet with margarine. 10. Place biscuits on baking sheet. 11. Bake 8 to 10 minutes until browned.

Prepare Topping

Ingredients:	*Utensils:*	*Directions:*
4 tablespoons sugar	small jar with cover	1. Measure sugar into jar.
2 teaspoons cinnamon	measuring spoons	2. Measure cinnamon into jar.
		3. Put on cover and shake until ingredients are well blended.

Cook Toast

Ingredients:	*Utensils:*	*Directions:*
2 slices bread	toaster	4. Cook bread in toaster.
2 teaspoons margarine	butter knife	5. Spread warm toast with margarine.
		6. Sprinkle toast with cinnamon-sugar mixture.

Garlic Rolls

2 servings

Preheat Oven to 375°

Prepare Bread

Ingredients:

2 crusty rolls

2 tablespoons margarine

garlic powder

Utensils:

bread knife

butter knife

Directions:

1. Slice rolls.

2. Spread margarine on each piece of roll.

3. Sprinkle with garlic powder.

Heat Bread

Utensils:

aluminum foil

Directions:

4. Wrap rolls in foil.

5. Put in oven 15 to 20 minutes or until warmed through.

Preheat Oven to 400°

Mix Batter

Ingredients:	Utensils:	Directions:
1 egg	mixing bowl	1. Break egg into bowl.
$\frac{1}{4}$ cup milk	measuring cup	2. Measure milk; add to bowl.
1 tablespoon vegetable oil	measuring spoons	3. Measure vegetable oil; add to bowl.
1 cup baking mix (such as Bisquick®)	mixing spoon	4. Mix together.
		5. Measure baking mix; add to bowl.
2 tablespoons sugar		6. Measure sugar; add to bowl.
		7. Stir just until moistened.

Bake Muffins

Utensils:	Directions:
muffin pan	8. Put 6 paper liners in muffin cups.
paper muffin liners	9. Spoon batter into muffin cups.
	10. Bake 15 to 18 minutes or until browned.

Variations

Blueberry Muffins: Add $\frac{1}{2}$ cup blueberries to batter before baking.

Apple Muffins: Add 1 chopped apple and $\frac{1}{4}$ teaspoon cinnamon to batter.

56

PART 6

Desserts

Apple Crisp

6 servings

Preheat Oven to 350°

Mix Topping

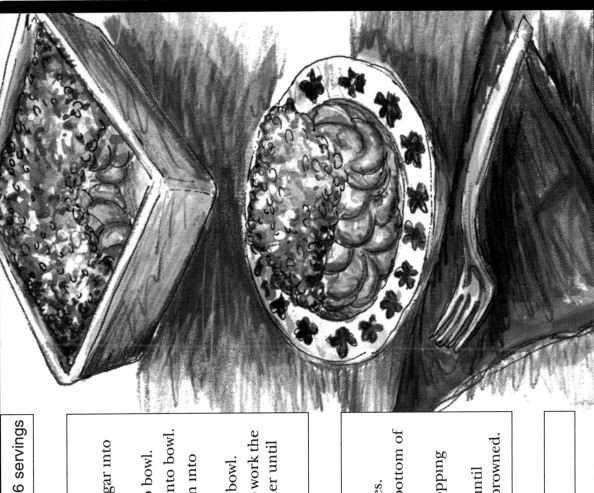

Ingredients:	Utensils:	Directions:
$\frac{3}{4}$ cup brown sugar	small bowl	1. Measure brown sugar into small bowl.
$\frac{1}{2}$ cup flour	measuring cup	2. Measure flour into bowl.
$\frac{1}{2}$ cup oatmeal	measuring spoons	3. Measure oatmeal into bowl.
$\frac{3}{4}$ teaspoon cinnamon		4. Measure cinnamon into bowl.
$\frac{1}{2}$ stick margarine, softened		5. Add margarine to bowl.
		6. Use your fingers to work the ingredients together until crumbly.

Assemble the Crisp

Ingredients:	Utensils:	Directions:
1 can apples	can opener	7. Open can of apples.
	square baking pan	8. Spread apples in bottom of pan.
	large spoon	9. Sprinkle crumb topping over apples.
		10. Bake 30 minutes until topping is lightly browned.

Variations

Use pears or peaches or other fruit instead of apples.

Preheat Oven to 375°

1 dozen cookies

Mix Batter

Ingredients:	Utensils:	Directions:
1 9-oz. package yellow cake mix 1 egg 1 tablespoon water $\frac{1}{2}$ cup chocolate chips	mixing bowl measuring spoons mixing spoon measuring cup	1. Empty cake mix into bowl. 2. Break egg into bowl. 3. Measure water into bowl. 4. Mix all ingredients together. 5. Measure chocolate chips; add to bowl; mix together.

Bake Cookies

	Utensils:	Directions:
	baking sheet spatula paper towel	6. Drop dough by the spoonful on baking sheet. 7. Bake 8 to 10 minutes or until cookies are browned. 8. Use spatula to place cookies on paper towel to cool.

Chocolate Cream Pie

6 servings

Mix Pudding

Ingredients:

1 package instant chocolate pudding mix (6 servings)

3 cups cold milk

Utensils:

mixing bowl

measuring cup

mixing spoon

Directions:

1. Empty pudding mix into bowl.

2. Add $\frac{1}{2}$ cup milk; mix well.

3. Gradually add the other $2\frac{1}{2}$ cups of milk; mix well.

Make Pie

Ingredients:

1 prepared graham cracker pie crust

whipped topping (such as Cool Whip®)

Directions:

4. Spread pudding in pie crust.

5. Top with whipped topping.

6. Keep in refrigerator until ready to serve.

Crispy Crunchy Bars

8 bars

Mix Ingredients

Ingredients:	Utensils:	Directions:
½ stick margarine 20 marshmallows 3 cups crisp rice cereal	saucepan wooden spoon measuring cup	1. Put margarine in saucepan. 2. Heat over medium heat until melted. 3. Add marshmallows to saucepan; stir until melted; remove from heat. 4. Measure cereal into saucepan; mix well.

Finish the Bars

Ingredients:	Utensils:	Directions:
½ teaspoon margarine	square baking pan knife	5. Grease pan with margarine. 6. Put mixture into square pan; press into place. 7. Refrigerate 2 to 3 hours. 8. Cut into 8 squares.

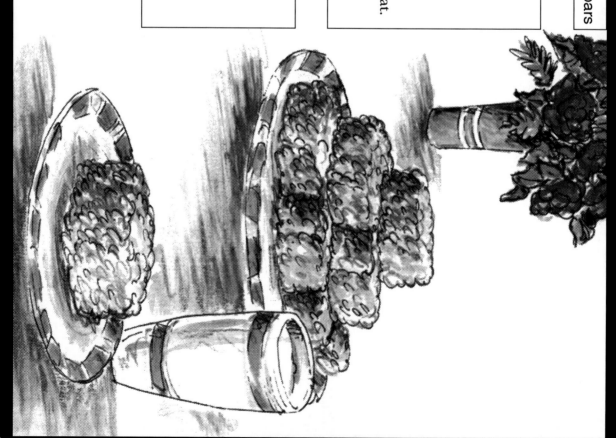

Fruity Gelatin

4 servings

Mix Gelatin

Ingredients:

1 package gelatin dessert (such as Jell-O®)

1 cup boiling water

4 ice cubes

1 8-oz. can fruit cocktail

Utensils:

mixing bowl

measuring cup

mixing spoon

can opener

Directions:

1. Empty package of gelatin into bowl.

2. Measure boiling water into bowl.

3. Mix until gelatin dissolves.

4. Add ice cubes to bowl; stir until melted.

5. Drain fruit cocktail; add juice to gelatin. (Set fruit aside.)

6. Put gelatin in refrigerator 30 to 45 minutes until it starts to thicken.

Add Fruit

Ingredients:

1 apple

whipped topping (such as Cool Whip®)

Utensils:

paring knife

cutting board

Directions:

7. Cut apple into 4 pieces; remove core; chop apple.

8. When gelatin starts to thicken, add apple and fruit cocktail.

9. Stir.

10. Refrigerate 2 to 3 hours until firm.

11. Serve with a spoonful of whipped topping.

1 dozen cookies

Mix Cookie Dough

Ingredients:	Utensils:	Directions:
1 cup sugar	saucepan	1. Measure sugar into saucepan.
$\frac{1}{2}$ stick margarine	measuring cup	2. Add margarine to saucepan.
$\frac{1}{4}$ cup milk	tablespoon	3. Measure milk and add to saucepan.
2 tablespoons cocoa	mixing spoon	4. Measure cocoa and add to saucepan.
2 tablespoons peanut butter		5. Mix ingredients.
$1\frac{1}{2}$ cups uncooked oatmeal		6. Place pan over medium heat; stir 2 or 3 times while cooking.
$\frac{1}{4}$ cup coconut		7. Boil 1 minute.
		8. Remove pan from heat.
		9. Measure peanut butter into saucepan.
		10. Measure oatmeal into saucepan.
		11. Measure coconut into saucepan.
		12. Stir until well mixed.

Shape Cookies

Utensils:	Directions:
wax paper	13. Place sheet of wax paper on table.
teaspoon	14. Use teaspoon to drop mixture onto the wax paper.
	15. Let cookies cool 2 to 3 hours.

Pudding Parfait

4 servings

Mix Pudding

Ingredients:

1 package instant vanilla pudding mix (4 servings)

2 cups cold milk

Utensils:

mixing bowl
measuring cup
mixing spoon

Directions:

1. Empty pudding mix into bowl.

2. Add $\frac{1}{4}$ cup milk; mix well.

3. Gradually add the other $1\frac{3}{4}$ cups milk; mix well.

Serve Pudding

Ingredients:

1 banana

whipped topping (such as Cool Whip®)

Utensils:

4 serving glasses
paring knife

Directions:

4. Put 2 spoonfuls of pudding in bottom of each glass.

5. Peel banana; slice half the banana into the serving glasses.

6. Add 2 more spoonfuls of pudding.

7. Slice other half of banana on the pudding.

8. Top with remaining pudding.

9. Keep in refrigerator until time to serve.

10. Just before serving, top with whipped topping.

Prepare Biscuits

Ingredients:		Directions:
2 biscuits		1. Make biscuits following directions on page 53, or purchase ready-made biscuits.

Prepare Filling

Ingredients:	Utensils:	Directions:
1 pint strawberries 2 tablespoons sugar	paring knife mixing bowl measuring spoons mixing spoon	2. Remove stems from strawberries. 3. Cut berries into small pieces. 4. Sprinkle sugar over berries. 5. Mix together.

Assemble Shortcakes

Ingredients:	Utensils:	Directions:
whipped topping (such as Cool Whip®)	2 dessert plates	6. Split biscuits in half and place on plates. 7. Spoon berries over biscuits. 8. Top with whipped topping.

Index

A

Apple(s)
    crisp, 59
    in fruit salad, 31
    in fruity gelatin, 63

B

Bagels
    pizza, 44

Baking mix such as Bisquick®
    for biscuits, 53
    for muffins, 56
    for pancakes, 12

Bananas
    in fruit salad, 31
    in pudding parfait, 65

Beans
    baked with pineapple and franks, 14
    green, in chicken noodle casserole, 3
    kidney, in chili, 5

Beef. *See also* Ground beef
    corned, in pocket sandwiches, 45
    oriental steak, 24
    pot roast, 26

Biscuits, 53
    in strawberry shortcake, 66

BLT sandwiches, 39

Bread
    biscuits, 53
    cinnamon toast, 54
    French toast, 9
    garlic rolls, 55
    muffins, 56

C

Cabbage
    in coleslaw, 30

Carrots
    in coleslaw, 30
    in pot roast, 26
    in tossed salad, 36

Casseroles
    chicken noodle, 3
    scalloped potatoes and ham, 15
    tuna, 20

Celery
    in chow mein, 6

Cheese
    in cheeseburgers, 40
    in grilled cheese sandwiches, 42
    mozzarella, with pizza bagels, 44
    in potato puffs, 29
    ricotta, in lasagna, 10
    ricotta, in stuffed baked potatoes, 35
    shredded, in pocket sandwiches, 45
    shredded, in tacos, 47
    in veggie hero sandwiches, 49

O

Onions
    in chow mein, 6
    in corn chowder, 8
    in meat loaf, 23
    in potato salad, 32

Open-faced turkey sandwiches, 43

Oranges
    in fruit salad, 31

Oregano
    in pizza bagels, 44
    in spaghetti sauce, 18

Oriental steak, 24

Oven-fried chicken, 25

P

Pancakes, 12

Parsley
    in egg salad sandwiches, 41
    in Spanish rice, 19

Pasta. *See* Noodles

Peach(es)
    crisp, 59
    in fruit salad, 31

Peanut butter
    in no-bake chocolate oatmeal cookies, 64

Pear(s)
    crisp, 59
    in fruit salad, 31

Peas
    in scalloped potatoes and ham, 15
    in tuna casserole, 20

Peppers, green
    in oriental steak, 24
    in potato salad, 32
    in tossed salad, 36
    in veggie hero sandwiches, 49

Pickles
    in pocket sandwiches, 45

Pies
    chicken, 4
    chocolate cream, 62
    shepherd's, 17

Pigs in a blanket, 13

Pineapple
    with baked beans and franks, 14

Pizza bagels, 44

Pocket sandwiches, 45

Pork
    in chow mein, 5

Pot roast, 26

Potato(es)
    cheesy potato puffs, 29
    chips, in tuna casserole, 20
    in corn chowder, 8
    in pot roast, 26
    salad, 32
    scalloped, with ham, 15
    in shepherd's pie, 17
    stuffed baked, 35

Pudding parfait, 65

R

Rice
    Spanish, 19